ADI 18.99/12.34

A STORY OF COURAGE

Laura Secord

Janet Lunn

Illustrated by Maxwell Newhouse

TUNDRA BOOKS

Published in Canada by Tundra Books,
481 University Avenue, Toronto, Ontario M5G 2E9

Published in the United States by Tundra Books of Northern New York,
P.O. Box 1030, Plattsburgh, New York 12901

First U.S. edition, 2002

Library of Congress Control Number: 2001087261

National Library of Canada Cataloguing in Publication Data

Lunn, Janet, 1928-
  Laura Secord : a story of courage

ISBN 0-88776-538-6

1. Secord, Laura, 1775-1868 – Juvenile fiction. 2. Canada – History – War of
1812 – Juvenile fiction.* I. Newhouse, Maxwell. II. Title.

PS8573.U55L38 2001   jC813'.54   C2001-930282-7
PZ7.L97912La 2001

We acknowledge the support of the Canada Council for the Arts and the
Ontario Arts Council for our publishing program.

We acknowledge the financial support of the Government of Canada
through the Book Publishing Industry Development Program for our
publishing activities.

Design: Sari Naworynski
Map: Malcolm Cullen
Medium: oil on board
Printed in Hong Kong

1 2 3 4 5 6   06 05 04 03 02 01

For Jeffrey with love
J. L.

In memory of my nephew Dale
M. N.

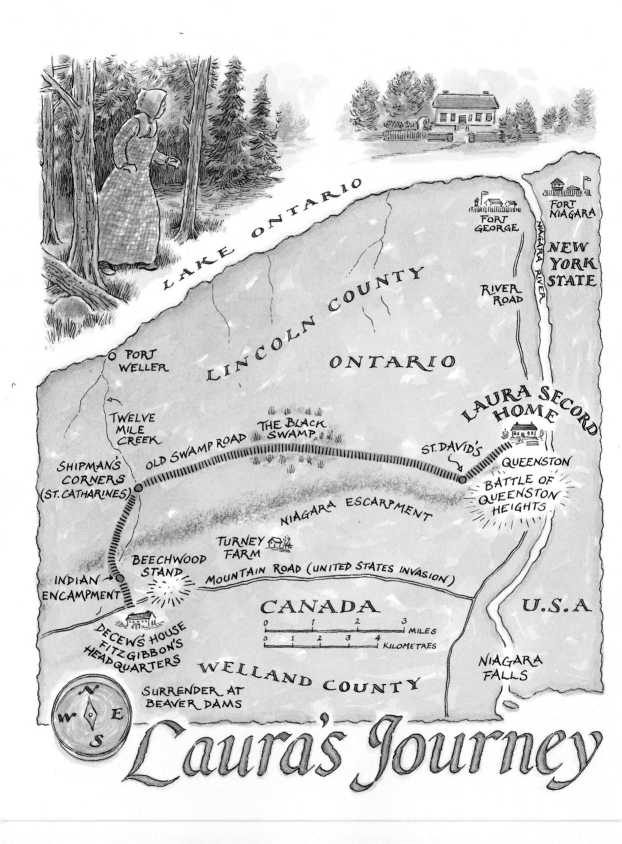

LAKE ONTARIO

FORT GEORGE

FORT NIAGARA

NIAGARA RIVER

NEW YORK STATE

RIVER ROAD

LINCOLN COUNTY

ONTARIO

O PORT WELLER

TWELVE MILE CREEK

THE BLACK SWAMP

ST. DAVID'S

LAURA SECORD HOME

OLD SWAMP ROAD

SHIPMAN'S CORNERS (ST. CATHARINES)

QUEENSTON

BATTLE OF QUEENSTON HEIGHTS

NIAGARA ESCARPMENT

TURNEY FARM

BEECHWOOD STAND

MOUNTAIN ROAD (UNITED STATES INVASION)

INDIAN ENCAMPMENT

DECEWS' HOUSE FITZGIBBON'S HEADQUARTERS

CANADA

U.S.A

0 1 2 3 MILES
0 1 2 3 4 KILOMETRES

WELLAND COUNTY

NIAGARA FALLS

SURRENDER AT BEAVER DAMS

N W E S

Laura's Journey

I

Laura Secord did not think of herself as a brave woman. She was gentle, a little shy, and soft spoken – and she looked it with her thoughtful dark eyes, her fair skin, and soft brown hair. Although she was slight and slim, she was strong. She could lift a heavy soap kettle. She could wield an axe. She could carry a bucket full of water, with a baby in one arm and at least one child hanging on to her skirt. She had a lot of energy, too. She could work from dawn until way past sunset before she got tired. But brave, no she didn't think she was that.

Laura *was* brave, though, and over many years her story has become one of Canada's great stories of courage. It's a story about the war of 1812 in Upper Canada, which is what Ontario was called back then. The war was between Great Britain and the United States. American political leaders were sure they would win the war and add British Canada to the United States. "It will be a mere matter of marching," they said. But it wasn't. For two years, from the summer of 1812 to the winter of 1814, fierce and bloody battles were fought on the Atlantic Ocean and on the lakes and rivers and surrounding land along the Canadian–American border.

Laura and her husband, James, lived in Upper Canada in the pioneer village of Queenston, where James was a storekeeper. They lived in a small white house with their five children: Mary, who was twelve; Charlotte, ten; Harriet, six; three-year-old Charles; and baby Appoloni.

Queenston was on the western bank of the Niagara River just across from Lewiston, New York in the United States. That meant that the Secords were in the thick of the war right from the start. James was a very proud Canadian and, the moment war was declared, he enlisted as a sergeant in the First Lincoln Militia. In fact, if General Brock, the commander of the British and Canadian forces, had said to him, "James Secord, you, and you alone, are to defend Upper Canada," James would likely have replied, "Yes, sir. I'll be glad to try."

In October of 1812, only four months after the war began,
James fought in the terrible battle on Queenston Heights
(a small, steep hill just above the Secords' own house). The
moment they heard the first gunshot, Laura and Fan, the servant
girl, gathered the children and ran for safety to an outlying farmhouse. All the women and children from the village were there.
Throughout the long day they sheltered in the house while the
cannons boomed, the muskets barked, and the bullets whistled
through their village. Those sounds and the sharp smell of
gunpowder that filled the air were dreadful, but the shouts and
screams of the fighting men were worse.

At last, in mid afternoon, the guns were silent and the smoke
began to clear. The British and Canadians, and their Iroquois and
Shawnee allies, had won the day. The enemy soldiers fled to their
boats or were taken prisoner. But the battle had cost dearly. Isaac
Brock, the beloved British general, was dead.

What Laura and the children found when they got home was
even harder to bear: their house had been looted and James
was missing.

"I've not seen him since the fight started early this morning,"
one of his tired comrades told Laura.

Not stopping for shawl or bonnet, Laura struggled up the hill through the trampled, blood-stained leaves. She peered into the face of every dead and wounded soldier until she found James. He was not dead but he had been shot in both a shoulder and a knee and he couldn't move. Frantically, Laura grabbed a man on his way down the hill. With his help, she got James home and into his own bed.

Before many weeks had passed, James's shoulder had healed, although it still caused him terrible pain. But a bullet had shattered his kneecap and, no matter what treatment the doctor ordered, no matter what Laura, Fan, or the older girls could do, it would not heal. He had to face the fact that his war service was over.

Laura's was still ahead of her.

2

There were no more battles in Queenston, but the war did not soon move from the Niagara District. American soldiers marched constantly through all the villages with their teams of horses and their heavy guns. Sometimes they burned houses. They barged into others demanding food, drink, and sleeping quarters. They helped themselves to whatever they wanted – dishes, silverware, furniture – anything. They looted the Secords' house twice. People were terrified, but there was nothing anyone could do but try to keep from being noticed.

In the spring of 1813, not a year after the Battle of Queenston Heights, there was a bloody battle at Stoney Creek, along the Lake Ontario shore. Neither side won, but the British and Canadians gained four military bases west of the Niagara River. The Americans held on to Fort George, at the mouth of the river, and the district as far as Queenston.

One hot, sultry evening in late June, an American officer pounded on the Secords' door demanding a meal for himself and his fellow officers. Laura knew better than to argue. She didn't say a word, but there was a glint of anger in her dark eyes and a grim set to her mouth. She ushered the officers into the kitchen and pulled out the benches around the big table.

"Put everything you have got on the table," she told Fan, "and set the whiskey jug out." Laura went outside to weed the kitchen garden.

The garden was not far from the kitchen window. Laura paid little attention to the soldiers until she heard one say, "FitzGibbon," in a loud, angry tone, then, "we've had enough of that fox! He's spiked our guns for the last time. General Boyd is right. We'll . . ." Here the officer lowered his voice, and Laura couldn't hear any more. James FitzGibbon was a British lieutenant who had been winning skirmishes against the American soldiers and making sport of their officers – perhaps the very ones sitting at Laura's kitchen table.

She crouched low beneath the sill. She listened as they talked in low voices about their general's plan to surprise Lieutenant FitzGibbon in his headquarters on Twelve Mile Creek, near Beaver Dams. "With 500 men surrounding that house," said one, "there'll be no escaping us this time." The others all laughed. Someone cheered. There was the sound of chairs scraping back against the kitchen floor.

Keeping down, Laura scurried away from the window and ducked behind the house. As soon as the thump of horses' hoof beats on the road had died away, she hiked up her skirts, flew into the house, up the stairs and into the bedroom to where her husband was resting on the bed. Breathlessly she told him what she'd heard. "James," she finished, shaking his arm, "Lieutenant FitzGibbon is our one big hope. Somebody must warn him."

Painfully, James sat up. He sighed. "Someone should," he said. "But who? If I crawled on my hands and knees, I could not get there in time."

For a moment Laura said nothing. "I…I could go," she said hesitantly.

"You go? The countryside between here and Beaver Dams is teeming with Yankees."

"That's so. It would be folly to take the straight road. I'd best go around by Shipman's Corners. I…"

"Lolly, FitzGibbon is headquartered at John DeCew's house. It must be twenty miles from here to DeCew's by Shipman's Corners. You would collapse in this heat."

"With God's help, I can do it," said Laura valiantly.

Cursing his own weakness, James said sternly, "Lolly, you are not to think of it." He stopped. "But you could walk as far as St. David's," he said slowly. "Your brother Charles is there at Hannah's. I know he's been ill, but he might be up and around by now. If not, I'll wager either one of Hannah's big boys would be as cocky as a cat in a cream dish to be asked to carry out a mission like this."

Laura slumped against the wall with a sigh of relief. One of Hannah's boys would go. She would not have to go all the way the DeCew's, only two miles to St. David's where James's widowed sister-in-law lived.

3

Before Mary and Charlotte went to bed that night, Laura told them that she was going to Aunt Hannah's early in the morning. "And you are to mind the young ones," she said, "and see to it there is no mischief and that there are no squabbles."

In the kitchen she asked Fan to make up a basket with a jar of yarrow tea for Charles's cough, a crock of berry preserve, a bit of butter, and "some of today's baking, if the American officers did not eat it all." That way she could show any enemy soldier who stopped her that she really was going to visit her sick brother.

The next morning, just before the sun came up, Laura was dressed and ready. She had pinned up her hair and put on a sunbonnet. She had dressed in her best cotton print gown and light slippers, just as she would if visiting Charles were all she meant to do. She kissed James goodbye, took the basket from the kitchen table, and slipped quietly through the front door. Out by the gate, she turned once to look back at the house where her family lay sleeping and was startled to see little Harriet watching from her bedroom window. Laura blew her daughter a kiss then started down the road.

To her relief, only the crowing roosters greeted her along the way. It had rained in the night and there was a cool breeze, so she swung along briskly. It wasn't yet breakfast time when she reached the Secord mill in St. David's and knocked on her sister-in-law's door. Hannah was surprised to see her and even more surprised to learn why she was there.

"Oh, Lolly!" She took the basket from Laura. "I'm afraid Charles is still feverish and the big boys have both gone off to join the militia. There are only Alex and Elizabeth here with me." Alex was Hannah's twelve-year-old son and Elizabeth her grown daughter.

"Well," Laura swallowed hard, "I will just have to go myself." She went upstairs to her brother while Hannah made breakfast. Then, while they ate, Hannah did her best to dissuade Laura from making the long walk.

"There's not another living soul to do it," Laura insisted and, reluctantly, Hannah gave up. She agreed that Laura would have to go around by Shipman's Corners where the countryside was in British hands.

Suddenly Elizabeth spoke up: "Aunt Lolly, I cannot let you go alone. I'm coming with you."

"No," said Laura. Elizabeth was not strong and Laura was sure that she could not stand up to a long, hard walk in such heat. Hannah didn't want her to go either, but neither did she want Laura to go alone. Elizabeth was determined and, in the end, Hannah kissed them both and wished them Godspeed.

4

The day was already hot. The road through the swamp was narrow and the dense cedar and willow branches overhead made it seem like a dark tunnel. It was still wet from the night's rain and smelled of mud and rotted plants. Both Laura and Elizabeth kept slipping into the slimy water. Their skirts were soon wet and heavy and their light slippers came off their feet countless times. The low-hanging branches scratched their hands and faces and, before they were halfway to Shipman's Corners, the steady croaking of the frogs and the infuriating hum of the mosquitoes were making them half frantic – and they were covered with bites.

Laura was so anxious to reach their destination and so afraid of enemy soldiers that she would have walked without stopping. But her niece tired easily and they had to rest often on rocks or fallen logs. Then, because Elizabeth was so sure there were rattle-snakes behind every tree and wild cats hunched on all the branches, she would jump to her feet almost at once and they would start off again.

By the time they reached the Shipmans' house at The Corners, Elizabeth was close to fainting, and Laura realized her neice could go no farther. Mrs. Shipman pulled them into the house without a word. She sat them down in her kitchen with tea and listened to their story. "Lord bless you," she said. Clucking like a mother hen, she put Elizabeth to bed at once. Laura ached for bed, too. Instead, she gratefully accepted another cup of tea and bit of bread and ham. Then she set out alone for John DeCew's house.

She was afraid to go by the road even though this was British territory, so Laura kept the westering sun to the right of her and followed Twelve Mile Creek as it wound its way South. As she plodded up and down hills, through woods and bramble thickets and across fields full of thistles and burdock, Laura told herself over and over again, "I *will* reach Lieutenant FitzGibbon."

It was afternoon by now and no breeze stirred the hot, humid air. She stopped once or twice to eat raspberries and blackcaps or to kneel by the creek to drink its water, but she was constantly on the lookout for wild animals and rattlesnakes. She was not as jumpy as her niece, but rattlesnakes were common and the story was told around every kitchen table in the Niagara District of how John DeCew had slept in a hammock to keep away from them when he'd built his first cabin.

It was deep twilight by the time she reached the rapids below DeCew's. She looked up to the ridge where she could just see the outline of the farmhouse. She closed her eyes for a moment in grateful prayer. She looked down at herself. The thought drifted through her mind that she was not properly dressed to meet an officer of His Majesty's army, and a tiny burst of laughter bubbled up inside her. She looked up – and found herself facing a whole party of Indians. They did not look friendly.

5

Shouting words in a language she did not understand, the Indians were moving towards her. One of them cried, "Woman!" She understood that. For an instant she almost sank to the ground in tears, but Laura had not come all this way to give up in a fit of weeping. Slowly she walked towards the men. She picked out the one she thought might be the chief, the one who had shouted "woman." Over the clamour of their voices, she said, loudly and clearly, "I have important news for Lieutenant FitzGibbon. You must let me pass."

"No," said the chief.

Laura wanted to stamp her foot. Instead she forced herself to speak calmly and firmly. "If you do not let me take this news to Lieutenant FitzGibbon, he and his men will all be killed," she said, "and probably you, too."

The chief shook his head. "No," he said again. Then, after a long pause, he asked her to give him the news she was bringing. Laura refused. He glared at her. There was a murmur of disapproval from his fellows. Finally he said, "Come," and, without another word, led the way up the hill to the house.

Lieutenant FitzGibbon looked up from his desk when Laura followed the chief into his office. He blinked. He shook his head. He stared. Before he could say a word, Laura spoke. "I have news for you," she said.

She told him everything she had heard from outside her kitchen window in Queenston. Lieutenant FitzGibbon said nothing for the longest time. He just sat and stared at her in disbelief. Then, with an exclamation of concern, he jumped to his feet and came around the desk. He took Laura by her arm and led her to a chair. "Find something for this woman to eat and drink," he ordered the guard at the door. "And when she's rested, I want her escorted to safety at Turney's."

The Turneys' farmhouse was just down the road from DeCew's, but when the British soldier lifted Laura down from his horse at the front door, she was almost asleep. She only dimly realized that she was being carried to an upstairs bedroom and being put to bed by Mrs. Turney.

She woke up two days later to the sight of Mrs. Turney's face and the smell of coffee. There was the sound of gunfire from outside the house.

While Laura slept, a battle had begun in a stand of beechwood trees near Beaver Dams almost outside her window.
It was the battle she had walked all that distance to warn
Lieutenant FitzGibbon about. The 500 American soldiers the
officer had bragged about in the Secords' kitchen had come to
surprise him and his 50 British soldiers. Because of Laura's
warning, the lieutenant was prepared and he sent his Mohawk
and Caughnawaga allies to turn the tables on the American
troops. He followed after with his 50 regular troops and fooled the
American colonel into believing that hundreds more were on
the way. The Americans surrendered. Laura's brave journey
through the wilderness had won the day for the British and their
Indian allies.

EPILOGUE

After the battle at Beaver Dams, the Americans retreated from
the Niagara District. The war continued until the winter of the
following year but it did not touch the district again. Neither the
British nor the Americans won the war. The only people who
really won were the Canadians. The boundary lines between
British North America and the United States remained unchanged.

Laura Secord returned home safely to her husband and children.
James never fully recovered from his wounds, his store had been
ruined and the jobs he found to do paid very little. The Secords
had two more children in the years after the war, and life was very
hard for the family with so little money.

Appoloni died when she was eighteen. All the other children
grew up and most of them married and had children of their own.
Hannah Secord's daughter, Elizabeth, died two years after the war.

James died when he was sixty-seven years old. Laura lived to be
ninety-three, but she received no recognition for her brave act
until many years after the war. Historians now believe that while
the war was still on, she was afraid of attracting attention from the
Americans to what she had done and so she kept it to herself. It was
a long time before the British and Canadian governments recognized
her heroism – or even believed that she had made that journey.

Eventually recognition came and, during the last years of her
life, Laura was much honoured. She was given a pension by the
Canadian government and three separate monuments were erected
in her memory: at Lundy's Lane, in Niagara Falls, and on Queenston
Heights. The Secord house in Queenston is now a museum.